the
SECRET WORLD
of WHALES

BY CHARLES SIEBERT
ILLUSTRATED BY MOLLY BAKER

DEVELOPED IN COLLABORATION WITH

NRDC

chronicle books · san francisco

TO BEX, ROZ, AND OLIVE
—C. S.

FOR BRAD
—M. B.

Image credits:
Page 28: Courtesy of the Library of Congress, LC-DIG-ppmsc-06256. Pages 30 to 31: From *Marine Mammals
of the Northwestern Coast of North America* by Charles Scammon (published in 1874). Page 33: (left) Ken Moore/
Dreamstime.com; (right) Jocrebbin/Dreamstime.com. Page 37: Courtesy of the Library of Congress, LC-
USZC2-1759. Page 38: (left) Courtesy of the National Oceanic and Atmospheric Administration/NEFSC, photo
by Peter Duley, research permit 775-1875; (right) Eric Isselée/Dreamstime.com. Page 41: Courtesy of the Library
of Congress, photo by Donald Hossack Bain, LC-USZ62-112949. Page 43: Courtesy of the Library of Congress,
Frank and Francis Carpenter Collection, LC-DIG-ppmsc-01648. Page 49: Sam Chadwick/Dreamstime.com.
Page 58: Toni Frohoff. Page 60: Courtesy of the National Oceanic and Atmospheric Administration/Depart-
ment of Commerce, from *An Account of the Arctic Regions with a History and Description of the Northern Whale-Fishery*
by W. Scoresby (published in 1820). Page 63: Courtesy of Jacob Scherr. Page 65: Courtesy of the National
Oceanic and Atmospheric Administration, Dr. Steven Swartz (NOAA/NMFS/OPR). Page 100: Leofrancini/
Dreamstime.com. Page 108: Courtesy of the National Oceanic and Atmospheric Administration.

All other photos: Shutterstock.com

Library of Congress Cataloging-in-Publication Data available.
ISBN 978-0-8118-7641-4

Book design by Molly Baker.
Typeset in Eureka and Oklahoma.

Manufactured by Toppan Leefung, Da Ling Shan Town, Dongguan, China,
in November 2010.

10 9 8 7 6 5 4 3 2 1

This product conforms to CPSIA 2008.

Chronicle Books LLC
680 Second Street, San Francisco, California 94107

www.chroniclekids.com

CONTENTS

In the spring of 2009, I traveled to the southwest coast of Baja, Mexico, in hopes of seeing my first whale in the wild. My first morning there, I sat in a small boat driven by a local guide named Ranulfo. I had just seen a huge mist of whale breath above the Pacific Ocean, and Ranulfo started steering in that direction. All at once the whale was leaping high up out of the sea and splashing down again. Ranulfo drove the boat faster and faster toward the whale, and then he suddenly shut the motor off.

"She's coming straight this way," he shouted.

My heart stopped, and before I knew what was happening, the whale surfaced right alongside us. She let out a huge, explosive breath of air and then went under again. Then, just moments later, she swam slowly up to the boat. That's when I saw the baby whale at her side: a young male already about as long as our boat and weighing at least two tons. He glided right toward us. When

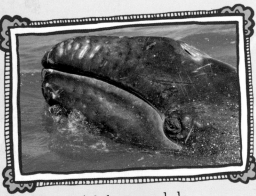

A baby gray whale

I looked over the edge, his huge head poked straight up out of the water, nearly bumping me in the nose.

I was now face-to-face with a baby whale. I could see my own reflection in the glassy brown orb of his huge oval eye. He floated there, watching me as though he was trying to figure out who and what I was. I will never forget it for as long as I live. I knew then that this was the closest I would ever come to meeting an extraterrestrial. And it happened right here on Earth.

I wrote this book to share the sense of wonder and awe I felt as I stared into the eye of that whale. In the pages ahead, you'll meet whales of all shapes and sizes. You'll read many of the whale myths and legends told over the ages, and you'll learn what the latest science is now revealing to us about these remarkable animals. You may also be inspired—I hope—to go out one day soon and have your own face-to-face encounter with a great whale. The experience will move you more than you can imagine. It might even make you want to join in the fight to protect whales and make tomorrow's oceans healthier places for them to live.

—CHARLES SIEBERT

BALEEN WHALES

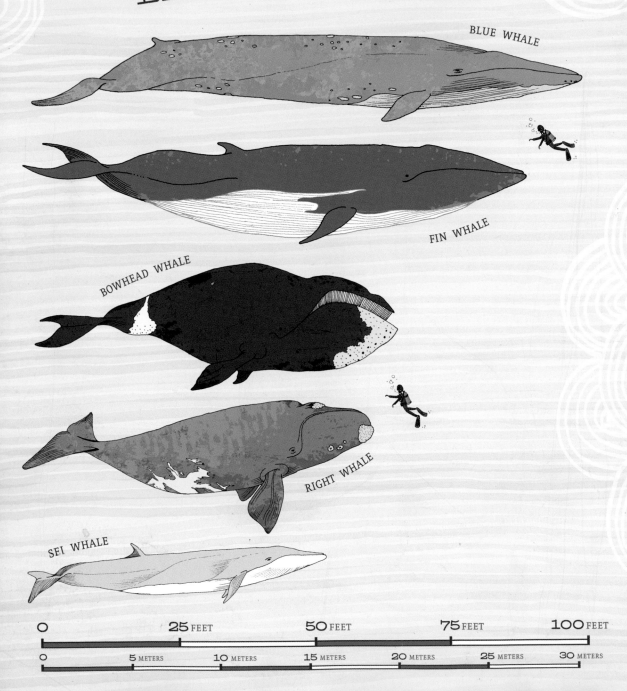

BLUE WHALE

FIN WHALE

BOWHEAD WHALE

RIGHT WHALE

SEI WHALE

0   25 FEET   50 FEET   75 FEET   100 FEET

0   5 METERS   10 METERS   15 METERS   20 METERS   25 METERS   30 METERS

GRAY WHALE

HUMPBACK WHALE

MEET *the* WHALES

TOOTHED WHALES

SPERM WHALE

ORCA (*Killer Whale*)

BELUGA WHALE (*White Whale*)

BEAKED WHALE

DOLPHIN

| 0 | 25 FEET | 50 FEET | 75 FEET | 100 FEET |

| 0 | 5 METERS | 10 METERS | 15 METERS | 20 METERS | 25 METERS | 30 METERS |

CHAPTER 1

TALES *of* WHALES

Long ago, people believed that the Earth was carried on the back of a whale. They also believed that all seven seas could fit inside one of the whale's nostrils, and that all earthquakes and floods were caused by the whale's sneeze.

It may be hard to imagine such things now. These days, whales are not as mysterious as they once were. We have all seen pictures of whales taken from passing boats and planes. We have made recordings of whale conversations and songs. Scientists have even followed whales with special cameras, swimming with them through their underwater world. We might think that we have, in every way, come to understand the whale. But we should think again.

OPPOSITE PAGE: The tail fin of a humpback whale

Imagine for a moment that you're a person from long ago, living on some lone and isolated seashore. You've lived your whole life never roaming farther than a day's walk from home. You have never met another human or any other animal beyond those in the immediate area of your own tribe. Then one day, not far off shore, something rises out of the water, something so gigantic, you think it's an island—until you realize it's breathing! And then it disappears again, leaving you without breath.

No wonder that people once thought whales were one and the same as the universe: huge, mysterious, immeasurable. The only possible way to capture such a creature back then was in stories.

WHALES AROUND THE WORLD

All around the world, from the barren Arctic to the lush tropical islands of the South Pacific, people who never knew of each other told strangely similar stories about the great whale, the terrific monster who both shaped and ruled the very fate of the world.

The ancient Chinese spoke of the whale as a huge dragonlike creature from the Northern Sea named Yu-kiang. Several thousand feet long, with the body of a fish and the hands and feet of a human being, Yu-kiang ruled over all the oceans. When it got angry, it turned into a gigantic bird that stirred the waters into terrifying storms.

The whale stories of the Inuit tribes of far northern Alaska also featured a huge bird. It was called Big Raven. One day, Big Raven came upon a whale lying helpless on the shore. As the Inuits believed that the Earth was carried on the back of a whale, it was very bad to find a whale stranded outside of the ocean, its natural home—it was a sign that the universe was in disorder.

Big Raven appealed to the Great Spirit of the sky to help him get the whale back to sea. The Great Spirit told

Big Raven of a certain place deep in the forest where at night moonlight fell in a magical way. Special mushrooms grew there, he was told, that if eaten, gave one tremendous strength. Big Raven found the spot and ate the mushrooms. Upon returning to the whale, he was able to drag him all alone back to sea and thus reestablish the proper order of things.

To the tribes of East Africa as well, the whale was one and the same as the world, put here by God to remind us of our small place in it. Once a great king named Solomon, proud of having fed all the people and animals of his kingdom, asked God if he could feed all the creatures on Earth. In response, God called forth from the sea a whale that rose up out of the water like a huge mountain. It ate all that King Solomon had to offer, then turned to him and cried, "I am still hungry. Feed me!" When the King asked the whale if there were more beings of his size in the sea, the whale replied, "Of my tribe there are seventy thousand!" and then the King understood the true enormity of the world and thanked the whale for allowing him to see it.

❧ THE GREAT LEVIATHAN ❧

In the Bible, there appears a whale-like creature known as the Leviathan, a great sea-monster as enormous, powerful, and mysterious as God. The Leviathan was capable, if disturbed, of swallowing the sun. This, many believed, was the cause of a solar eclipse.

Since the Leviathan was thought to be the Earth's very foundation, many believed that earthquakes were caused when the devil tempted the creature to throw off the Earth by wriggling its back.

⚜ THE WHALE ISLAND ⚞

From the very beginning of travel by sea, the same story is told time and again. A ship comes upon a dark, uncharted island. The crew throws down an anchor, ties up the vessel, and then everyone goes about setting up camp, only to find that their "island" is suddenly moving. Why? It's a whale!

One of the earliest recorded versions of the "whale island" tale can be found in a collection of stories from ancient Greece in the second century. "There is a certain whale in the sea called Aspidoceleon, that is exceedingly large," the tale begins. "Ignorant sailors tie their ships to the beast as to an island and plant their anchors and stakes in it. They light their cooking fires on the whale, but when it feels the heat it . . . plunges into the depths, sinking all the ships."

Three centuries after the story of the Greek sailors, there was one about an Irish monk named Saint Brendan. He and 17 fellow monks traveled far and wide around the British Isles and along the coast of France. One Easter Sunday, Brendan and his companions set foot on a barren, unknown island to worship. While Brendan prayed at a makeshift altar, the other monks built a fire in a cauldron to cook their breakfast. All at once, the ground began to stir and quake beneath them. Upon scrambling back to their boat, they turned around in time to see their island, a great whale that Brendan would later name Jasconius, swimming away, the smoldering remains of their breakfast fire disappearing over the horizon.

It all might sound like something out of a dream, and yet how is it that so many different sailors from different times and distant places could have the same dream?

The whale-island tale makes perhaps its earliest appearance in the Talmud, the ancient text of Jewish law, customs, and history. Some scholars trace it back to the folklore of ancient India and Persia, which would explain why it also turns up many centuries later in the famous collection of Persian folk tales known as *The Thousand and One Nights*, starring, among others, a sailor named Sinbad.

On the first of his seven voyages, Sinbad sets out into the Persian Gulf. When the wind suddenly drops, Sinbad and his fellow travelers find themselves

adrift near a small island that resembles a green meadow rising slightly above the surface of the water. The ship's captain gives permission for all who wish it to go ashore for a while and amuse themselves. Sinbad and a handful of others stroll about on the island for a time, then light a fire and are sitting down to enjoy a meal when they are startled by a sudden and violent trembling. Looking back toward the ship, they see those on board screaming at them to come fast, and they all start running for their lives, realizing that the ground beneath them is nothing but the back of a sleeping whale.

〰 SWALLOWED BY A WHALE 〰

If mistaking a whale for an island sounds crazy, what about being swallowed by a whale—and living to tell the tale?

Such stories were as common as those about whale islands. The thought of being swallowed by a whale haunted seafarers for centuries. The great whale of old legends was, after all, as wide as the whole universe and as long as all time. To be inside of him would have seemed like tumbling through eternal space. To come out alive again would have been like being reborn.

Among the Bible's best-known tales is that of the prophet Jonah, whom God sends to save the city of Nineveh from its own wickedness. When Jonah attempts to avoid the task and escape by ship, God sends a great storm to stir up the sea. Thrown from his ship and near drowning, Jonah calls out for God to save him. Instead, a great whale arrives and swallows up Jonah. After three days and nights of praying within the dark and vaulted chambers of the whale's belly, Jonah is spit out again into daylight and dry land, reformed and ready to take on his original mission.

Could someone really survive in the belly of a whale? No one can say for certain. But the great size and slowness of the whale's digestive system has certainly inspired the imaginations of seamen over the years. In 1891, it was reported that a man named James Bartley fell out of his ship near the Falkland Islands off the coast of Argentina and got swallowed by a sperm whale. The whale was supposedly captured the very next day by Bartley's shipmates, who quickly cut him free on the ship's deck. Bartley lived, or so the story goes, but he went a bit crazy and took months to recover his senses.

Sailors are famous, of course, for their "tall tales" (wild, made-up stories). It is often said that they tell them in order to keep the night watchmen awake. But the story that a longtime harpooner from Yorkshire named Bully Sprague would tell his shipmates was a real whopper. He spoke of the time that he was swallowed by an old sperm whale named Timor Tom. Once inside, Bully calmly sat on the whale's liver and lit a pipe. After a time, Bully noticed Timor Tom wasn't at all accustomed to tobacco. So he decided to take some of the tobacco leaves he had in his side pouch, roll them up, and place them in the lining of the whale's stomach.

"The whale began heavin' an' squirmin' real awful," Bully recounted, "when, all at once, the stomach turned clean over with a flop like an earthquake. . . ."

Bully went on to describe being spit out of the sick whale's mouth with a pile of chewed-up squid.

Just as remarkable as Bully's exit from the whale, however, was what he claimed to have discovered while he was still inside of it. Prior to making his clever escape, Bully used the light of a jellyfish to inspect his surroundings. He soon learned that he wasn't the first of Timor Tom's unwilling guests. Etched there, like graffiti, on the inner walls of the old whale's stomach were the words JONAH, 1683 B.C.

 WALK INSIDE A WHALE

Long ago, whenever people came upon the great Leviathan stranded onshore, they had no way to put it back in the ocean again. Without the magical mushrooms that aided Big Raven or the modern machinery of today, they could not move the dying whale. But later, once the great animal had died, they did move its bones. They took its high-arching rib bones and its back and jaw bones and brought them inside places of worship to pray beside.

In churches all over Europe, whale bones were hung. Sometimes the whale itself became the house of worship. In ancient Rome, during the reign of the Emperor Septimus Severus, a giant whale was stranded on the shores of the Tiber River. A model was promptly made of it and crafted into a theater for wild animal shows. People traveled from all over the Mediterranean to walk inside the whale model. Seated within the whale's great ribbed chest and belly, they'd watch the spectacle of wild bears, boars, elephants, and lions all being marched in through the whale's propped-open mouth.

This same tradition lasted until as recently as a hundred years ago. In cities and towns across Europe and America, people could walk inside the preserved bodies of actual stranded whales. In 1865, a blue whale, the largest of all the whales on Earth, was stranded off the coast of Sweden. The body was preserved and converted into a traveling whale café that was taken to major cities across Europe. People would stroll in through the whale's opened mouth. They'd

have tea or coffee inside the curved, candlelit walls of the whale's belly. And then they would reemerge, just like Jonah and the others, back into the light of day.

The next time you step inside a cathedral, a great government building, or a museum, look up into their high arches, domes, and ceiling vaults. Those were not things we just made up out of thin air. They were inspired by what Jonah, and James Bartley, and Bully Sprague, and who knows how many others, all saw when they first looked up, in both fear and wonder, inside the belly of the whale.

CHAPTER 2

WHALE HUNTING

Who would dare to hunt the great whale?

No one really knows who the first person was to have such a crazy idea. The best anyone can guess is that it all started when a sick whale, or an old and dying one, suddenly found itself washed up onshore. In the sea, a whale has no idea how massive and heavy it actually is. When it's underwater, a whale is like a giant hot air balloon adrift above the earth. It swims along on the ocean's currents, often going for thousands of miles without rest. On land, however, a whale comes crashing down hard; its bones and lungs soon collapse under the tremendous weight of its own mountainous flesh.

OPPOSITE PAGE: A whaling boat in Norway in the 1890s

Such a creature lying onshore would have inspired great wonder. But to a hungry local tribesman, looking to feed himself and his fellow villagers, a stranded whale was also dinner, and lots of it. One large whale could supply enough blubber, meat, and drinkable whale oil to get an entire village through a cold, harsh winter, sometimes with enough left over to trade with nearby villages.

It wasn't long before the taste for whale had hunters going off to sea in search of fresh meat. This same impulse arose all over the world, wherever land and sea meet. On a sandstone cave wall in South Korea, a drawing more than 8,000 years old shows a boatload of tiny human figures hunting a huge whale. Sperm whales were hunted in the Indian Ocean far off the coast of East Africa. Right whales were taken when they came to breed off the coast of what is now Florida. Bowhead whales were chased off the Arctic shores of Siberia. In the North Pacific, gray whales, humpbacks, and fin whales were all hunted.

Each local native culture would develop its own method of capturing whales. Some used darts dipped in plant poisons.

Others trapped whales in shallow bays. But by far the most important invention for hunters—and the worst possible news for whales—was the harpoon.

🐚 THE DEADLY HARPOON 🐚

Harpoons were long spears with pointed tips that had jagged toothlike barbs on them. The barbs made sure the spearhead would remain inside the whale's flesh. The harpoon itself would not kill the whale. Instead, the harpoon had a long rope attached to it, and fishermen would hold on to the rope. The whale would drag the hunters and their boat until it was exhausted. A final fatal blow was then struck with a lance to the whale's body.

Sometimes whales reacted to the first harpoon attack by trying to dive toward the ocean floor. So the hunters would also attach floats to the line to create more drag and help prevent the whale from pulling them and their boat underwater.

Making the equipment for whaling expeditions was a great challenge in itself. Early hunters had to make use of whatever local materials happened to be available. The harpoons used by East African whalers, for example, were the same type of wood and stone-tipped spears that local tribesmen used 40,000 years ago to hunt the hippopotamus. In the Pacific Northwest, along the coasts of what are now Oregon and Washington and British Columbia, harpoon heads were often made out of elk horn. They were fastened to the end of a wooden spear shaft with the dried tendons of sea lions. For the barbs on the harpoon head, sharp mussel shells would be glued along the edges of the elk-horn tip with the sticky sap from spruce trees.

⚓ MADE FROM A WHALE ⚓

As humans got better at hunting, the supply of whale meat became steadier, and permanent settlements formed. This gave people the leisure time to make even better whale-hunting tools and to find other uses for the whales' remains. Entire civilizations were built on the parts of whales. People lived

BALEEN

in houses built out of whale rib bones. They were buried in coffins made out of whale jaws and shoulder blades.

One very important part of the whale is the baleen—the flexible and durable plates that some whales use to catch tiny sea creatures in their mouths. Villagers made everything from hair combs to toboggans out of baleen. They also used it to build the ribbed frames of kayaks, which were then

WHALE "NOSE" WITH BARNACLES

BALEEN

Whales use the baleen to "filter feed." They take a big gulp of seawater, and the baleen acts like a filter, catching tiny sea creatures like plankton, krill, and small fish.

Baleen is made of keratin, the same substance found in your fingernails and hair.

covered with stretched seal skin. This made for supple, easily maneuvered vessels, ideal for hunting more whales.

❦ THE WHALE'S WORST ENEMY ❧

Of all the people who hunted whales around the world, nobody was more skilled than the Basque, a rugged group of fishermen and shepherds from the north of Spain. The very word *harpoon* comes from *arpoi*, a native Basque term that means "to take quickly." Back in the Middle Ages, the Basque built special stone viewing towers called "vigas" along the Bay of Biscay, the right whale's winter breeding grounds. Whenever a great spout of right whale breath, known as a "blow," was sighted above the sea, a bell would ring out from the viga, and a crew of six oarsmen, a captain, and one harpooner, would rush to their 25-foot-long (7.6-meter-long) hunting boats, known as "chalupas."

The right whale, like the bowhead, is a large, slow-swimming whale whose body, conveniently, floats to the surface after being killed. This made it the "right whale" for hunting. Once the Basque whalers reached the side of their slow-moving prey, the harpooner would thrust the sharp, barbed harpoon deep into the whale. As the wounded whale dove, the crew tied the line to their boat and followed along on the water's surface, waiting for the whale to emerge again for its next breath. Another whaler would then strike with a lance, and the floating body could be easily rowed back to shore.

THE DAWN OF THE WHALE INDUSTRY

The Basque turned whale hunting into an industry. By the thirteenth century, European countries were getting whatever whale products they wanted through trade with the Basque.

Whale meat became a regular part of Catholic Europe's diet on Fridays and during Lent when red meat couldn't be eaten. Whale tongue was considered a delicacy among the wealthy, and the lower classes ate a salt-cured form of whale meat much like bacon. Boiled whale blubber was made into oil to light dark castles, town squares, and peasant huts. It was also used to lubricate tools, early machines, and weaponry, and to make soap. Whale bones, baleen, and skin were used for everything from crafting fence posts to making whips and fishing rods and shoes. And when other European nations started getting involved in whaling, who did they hire? Who else but the Basque.

By the early 1600s, with few whales left in the Bay of Biscay, the Basque had to go in search of other whales in other parts of the Atlantic. This led them to invent a new kind of whaling. They built a larger ship that could take smaller whaling boats and their crews with it. They would then sail to wherever the whales were and launch the whaleboats from the big ship. The Basque were soon roaming as far as Greenland and then to the northeast coast of North America. They hunted right whales and bowheads along the way, then towed them to the nearest shore to boil the blubber down into precious oil. There is one spot along the northeast coast of Canada where the Basque boiled down the blubber of so many captured whales that, to this day, more than 400 years later, the ground there still feels oily.

Soon Denmark, Holland, England, Germany, and France were all sending out whaling fleets of their own. Later, the early American colonies started to get in on the action as well. Then, one day back in 1712, outside the busy whaling port of Nantucket, Massachusetts, the whaling industry and the world were changed forever.

Whalers attack a right whale.

A NEW KIND OF WHALE

While making his way in his ship along the southern coast of Massachusetts, Captain Christopher Hussey and his crew suddenly found themselves being swept by stiff winds out to sea. There they soon noticed a series of oddly shaped blows. The right whale's blow comes out in two prongs like a V. This one came out in a single, crooked line. Steering furiously in the direction of the strange blow, Hussey and his crew soon found themselves face-to-face with a massive sperm whale.

V-SHAPED RIGHT
WHALE BLOW

SPERM WHALE BLOW

Sperm whales have huge, fist-shaped heads and a very long, thin lower jaw with rows of teeth. Moby-Dick, Herman Melville's famous fictional white whale, was a sperm whale (an albino one). Sperm whales are the largest of the toothed whales, a family that also includes orcas (killer whales) and dolphins.

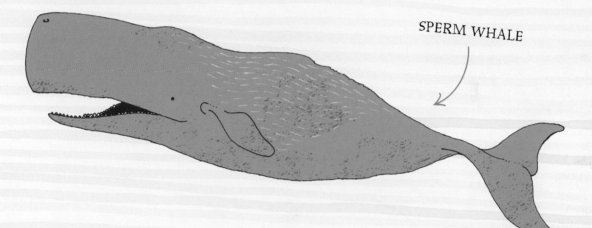

SPERM WHALE

Sperm whales don't have baleen. But, as Captain Hussey and his men soon discovered when they managed to haul their catch back to shore that day, sperm whales have other things that are just as valuable. First, their oil is far more pure and clean-burning than that of other whales. Then, inside of the sperm whale's head cavity, there is a thick, liquid substance called "spermaceti." When exposed to the outside air, this liquid turns to a solid wax—the finest anyone had ever seen. It produces a bright, clear flame with little smoke.

Unlike the other whales hunted until then, the sperm whale swam far offshore and mostly in warmer tropical waters. Capturing them required long ocean voyages. The warmer weather also meant that the blubber of a killed whale would rot before it could be brought back to shore to be boiled down into oil. American whalers soon solved the problem by installing brick ovens on ships. The blubber was turned to oil right on deck and then stored in wooden casks that were delivered back to the newly established whaling port of New Bedford, Massachusetts.

By the time the colonies declared independence in 1776, American whalers were already sending four times more oil to England than British whalers were. By the mid 1800s, the little town of New Bedford had dispersed so much whale oil and wax, it became known as "the city that lit the world."

A WHALE-POWERED WORLD

Whaling ships had now become little floating factories. Soon, even faster steam-powered whaling ships were being built, equipped with new explosive harpoons, and automatic wenches for hauling whales on deck. Sperm whales, right

Captured and killed whales hauled ashore around 1900

whales, bowheads, and gray whales were all being slaughtered by the thousands wherever ships could find them. By the time these ships made it back to port, whatever whales had been captured had already been broken down into different parts, and those parts were running the world.

Along with the lighting for homes and shops, whale oil greased the great machines of industry. It also went into soap, paint, varnish, and cosmetics. Baleen was like the world's first plastic. It was everywhere you looked: the spines of umbrellas, the shock absorbers of carriages, the whips of the carriage driver, the hoops of women's skirts, and the ribs of their corsets. Fishing rods, canes, tongue scrapers, combs, and shoehorns were all made from baleen. The finer, frayed edges of baleen plates went into brooms and chimney brushes and even formed the little springs in some of the world's first typewriters. Shop and inn owners painted signs on the wide surface of whale shoulder blades. Whale teeth were fashioned into jewelry, chess pieces, and piano keys.

Great Leviathan, the once-mysterious master of the seas, had allowed us to master life on land. The question was, how much longer could our way of life depend on whales before theirs was destroyed altogether?

Workmen cut up a captured blue whale in Alaska in the early twentieth century.

CHAPTER 3

RUNNING OUT of WHALES

Whales helped us to advance technology, and technology helped us kill more whales. By the beginning of the twentieth century, faster and more powerful whaling ships could hunt their prey in the world's remotest corners. They were even tapping into the Antarctic feeding grounds of the still plentiful fin whales and sei whales, and the blue whale, the Earth's largest creature.

The whalers, meanwhile, no longer needed to leave their ships and risk their lives in smaller boats. Harpoons were shot out of cannons and traveled more than 150 feet (45 meters). They would explode on contact, setting star-shaped barbs deep into the whales' flesh. By the 1920s, whaling ships were even using sonar (SOund NAvigation Ranging), a location technology using sound waves first developed during World War I to find and track enemy submarines. Diesel engines were introduced around that same time and spotter planes came into use to track whales as well. The animals didn't stand a chance.

With the discovery of petroleum beneath the ground in 1859 and the invention of the lightbulb a short time later, whale oil was no longer needed for lamps. And steel and plastic would soon replace baleen. But we found other uses for Leviathan. Whale oil went into plant fertilizer, margarine, and cosmetics. Whale meat was being made into dog food and in some countries, like Japan, it was served in restaurants.

Whales of all types and ages, from adults to newborns, were now being hunted. And because all the cutting up and preparing of the different parts was done on the ships, people onshore had no idea that so many whales were being slaughtered. In the North Atlantic, the gray whale had already been hunted out of existence, and the right and bowhead whales were close behind. On the west coast of the United States and along far-eastern shores of Japan and Siberia, the gray whale was rapidly disappearing as well. The world was fast running out of whales, and the whaling industry knew something had to be done.

THE INTERNATIONAL WHALING COMMISSION

In 1931, a year in which more than 30,000 blue whales alone were killed, the League of Nations, the forerunner of today's United Nations, announced the Convention for the Regulation of Whaling. Six years later, the three most endangered species, Pacific grays, bowheads, and right whales, were the first to be officially listed for protection. Then, in 1946, the Convention for the Regulation of Whaling established the International Whaling Commission (IWC) to begin placing limits on whale hunting worldwide. This was being done more out of concern for the future of whaling than for the well-being of whales. The belief was that regulation would allow whale populations to rebound. The reality, however, proved to be far different.

The IWC had little influence on the industry. When the Arctic was hunted dry, whaling ships focused on southern waters. By the late 1950s, it was estimated that more than 350,000 blue whales had been killed in the twentieth century alone, leaving only 4,000 or so remaining. By the mid-1960s, humpback whales had been nearly wiped out, and with 30,000 fin whales being caught each year, their numbers were dwindling fast.

A team of scientists from the United States, Britain, and New Zealand was commissioned in 1960 to do a survey of whale populations, and they arrived at some startling figures. There were thought to be fewer than a thousand blue whales left in the world. Humpback numbers were found to be so low that even with a complete ban on their hunting, the scientists estimated it would take nearly a century for their population to fully recover.

The biggest problem was that whalers didn't believe the scientists' figures. They also didn't believe that other countries were obeying the limits set by the IWC. In the late 1980s, Russian scientists revealed that whaling fleets under the former Soviet Union had been cheating since the IWC was first formed.

In 1986, the IWC imposed a ban on all whale hunting, but Japan and Norway found ways to dodge the rules and keep whaling. Both countries continue hunting whales to this day, despite the protests of environmental groups.

A BRIGHTER FUTURE?

The current outlook for the world's whales is uncertain. Some species have shown signs of recovery since the IWC's 1986 whale-hunting ban. The Pacific gray whale population, for example, is estimated to be around 20,000 now. But while some progress has been made, whale populations all over the world are still considered threatened.

And yet even as whale hunting continues in some parts of the world, there are signs that humans are entering a new era in their relationship with whales. Whale watching has become a very popular activity. People are willing to pay quite a bit of money to go for a ride on a boat in the hopes of seeing a whale. If this trend continues, the world's remaining whale hunters may decide that they'd be better off running a whale-*watching* business instead of a whale-killing business!

The popularity of whale-watching tours is a positive development for whales and people. It is a sign that we have begun to marvel at whales again, just as early man did. But this time around, our awe is inspired not by fear, but by knowledge.

Whale watchers in Alaska see a humpback whale.

CHAPTER 4

THE EARLY SCIENCE *of* WHALES

For much of the twentieth century, scientific research on whales was done mostly to help with whale hunting. Scientists studied whales from planes, following them on their migration routes and doing population counts. Studies were also done of the age, condition, and stomach contents of killed whales in order to figure out how healthy the whale populations were and how much of each species could be hunted.

Some early research was done simply to learn about the whales, but the methods were often as brutal as those used by hunters.

OPPOSITE PAGE: A humpback whale

In 1956, a cardiologist named Paul White traveled to Baja, Mexico, to get the first-ever recording of a whale's heartbeat. This required implanting a harpoon with an attached electrical monitoring device directly into the whale's heart. The harpoon eventually killed the whale, but not before revealing that a whale's heart works very much like our own.

And, as scientists would soon learn, the whale heart fuels a brain that also works much like our own.

Around the same time as Dr. White's heart experiment, biologists began using hydrophones (underwater microphones) to record the sounds whales make. A sound specialist named William Schevill made the first underwater recordings of whales in the wild. He recorded a number of baleen whale species, sperm whales, and one of the smaller members of the toothed whale family, the dolphin. No one was quite sure at the time what these sounds were for. But one early hint came from our own underwater sound technology, sonar, which involves sending out pulses of sound and then measuring how long it takes for the sounds to echo back. Sonar has long been used for determining the ocean's depth and for finding submarines. We even used it to find whales.

BLIPS IN THE OCEAN

In the 1950s, there was a period of intense rivalry and suspicion between the United States and Russia. During this time, the U.S. Navy began to detect a steady series of electronic-sounding blips in the ocean. The suspicion was that the Russians were using sonar to locate our submarines. The Russians denied the accusation, and the tensions mounted.

With the use of his hydrophone equipment, William Schevill was able to locate the sounds' mysterious source. It turned out they were coming from fin whales. As fin whales make their way to the surface to breathe, they emit a steady series of *blip* sounds that last for as long as fifteen minutes.

It began to dawn on everyone that whales seemed to have their own built-in sonar. In the dark depths of the sea, the whales were using these sounds to navigate—allowing them to determine the ocean's depth, or the size and shape of potential predators or prey. The process is known as "echolocation," that is, listening to echoes that have bounced off an object to figure out that object's size and location. And yet, as future research would reveal, whale sounds are used for much more than just echolocation.

❧ HUMPBACK SONGS ❧

In 1967, biologist Roger Payne recorded hundreds of hours of humpback whale sounds in the humpbacks' breeding grounds off the coast of Bermuda. After many long hours spent listening to the tapes, Payne began to notice that he was hearing more than just random noise. He recognized the same sequences and patterns of sounds. He heard internal rhythms and refrains not unlike those found in human music.

Whales evolved many millions of years before we humans even arrived on the scene, so their songs are far older than ours. In fact, whales are perhaps nature's oldest songwriters!

Payne's recordings were released in 1970 as a record album entitled *Songs of the Humpback Whale*. The record became an overnight worldwide sensation, and had a huge effect on how people thought about whales. Listening to the songs of

humpbacks alone in a dark room—the eerie squeaks and long, drawn-out moans—instantly transports you into the vast, dark chat room that is the whale's underwater world.

⚓ BEATS, CLICKS, MOANS, AND GARGLES ⚓

Recordings have since been made of many other whale species. Gray whales sound like they're banging on conga drums. Sperm whales make loud sequences of clicks that begin in their huge head cavities and then echo across miles of ocean. The blue whale produces the loudest sounds of any living creature on the planet, and yet we humans can't even hear them. Their deep moans and gargling sounds, which register at four octaves below the range of human hearing, travel more than 2,000 miles (3,220 kilometers), practically from one side of the ocean to the other!

Think about it. For millions of years before we humans came along and invented our own way of talking, whales were down there under the sea, using their own language, singing their own songs—not yet interrupted by our noises, or fishing nets, or harpoons.

⚒ WHALES IN SPACE ⚒

In 1977, the *Voyager 1* and *Voyager 2* spacecrafts began their endless journeys into the far reaches of outer space. Attached to the side of each spacecraft is a gold-plated copper disc containing digital images and sounds that were selected to portray the diversity of life and culture here on Earth. Among the sound recordings are greetings in 55 different languages, the beating of a human heart, the chirping of birds and crickets, and the songs of the humpback whale.

When we first launched those discs into outer space, the hope was that they would one day be intercepted by some other intelligent life-form. What we didn't fully realize at the time, however, is that such extraterrestrial intelligences were living right here beside us all along, adrift in their own separate underwater civilization.

CHAPTER 5

OUR ENCOUNTERS *with* WHALES

On a February morning back in 1972, something very strange happened in a lagoon in Baja, Mexico. A young fisherman named Francisco "Pachico" Mayoral set out in his small motorboat with his partner, Santo Luis Perez. They were out on the lagoon's calm, clear waters, dropping their nets to catch sea bass, when all at once, a massive 30-ton female gray whale approached their boat.

Pachico tried to steer away, but the whale kept following them. At one point, the whale went right under the boat and circled back toward them. Pachico turned off the motor, and he and his partner just sat there, perfectly still, terrified of what might happen next.

OPPOSITE PAGE:
An encounter with a baby gray whale in Baja, Mexico

Their fear was understandable. The gray whales of Baja had come to be known over the years as the "hardheaded devil fish," because they would do anything to protect their young from hunters, often rising up out of the water to smash whaling boats and drown their occupants. The hunting of gray whales had been banned in 1937. Still, even 35 years later, the whales were known to attack boats, and fishermen like Pachico were careful to keep their distance from the "devil fish." They knew a gray whale could destroy one of their boats with one swipe of its powerful tail.

Pachico had good reason to expect the worst as the huge gray whale kept circling around his boat that February morning. Then she came underneath the boat again. This time, however, she paused and rose up out of the water, balancing the boat on her back. There were Pachico and his partner, just like Sinbad and all those other sailors in the ancient stories, stranded on top of a giant whale island.

But instead of being tossed into the air, their boat was gently set back down in the water again. And then the whale came around once more and popped up out of the water directly beside the boat. She held there for so long, her huge whale eye staring at Pachico, that his fear began to dissolve away. When he finally decided to reach over with a finger and touch the whale on her head, she let him. Pachico then placed his whole hand on her, petting her, and she held there still, as though enjoying this new kind of contact with humans—the tender, friendly kind.

News of Pachico's extraordinary encounter spread fast among the local fishing villages of Baja. No one knew quite what to think of it. Some found the story hard to believe. But Pachico began taking more and more people out on the lagoons, and they too had similar encounters. Somehow, despite all the years of brutal hunting, the whales seemed to have changed their attitude toward human beings. Indeed, within a few years of Pachico's close encounter, the villagers had replaced the term "devil fish" with *ballenas amistosas*, Spanish for "friendly whales."

❧ MEET THE FRIENDLIES ❧

Now, every late winter and early spring when the gray whales come to Baja to give birth and nurse their young, Pachico and other fishermen in the area work as guides, taking tourists out on the lagoons to have their own encounters with the "friendlies." Thousands come every year from around the world and are amazed to see whale mothers guiding their newborn calves right up to boats so people can reach over and pat their rubbery heads. Often the whales will open their mouths wide and let people rub their tongues and baleen.

No one is exactly sure how to explain this behavior. It is not as if the whales are hungry and looking for food. Gray whales mostly eat tiny sea creatures called krill that they sift from the ocean floor, and people in the whale-watching boats are not allowed to feed the whales anyway. Some have claimed that the whales are merely attracted by the sounds of the boat motors, or that they like to rub their backs against the bottoms of boats to scratch their itches and to remove the hard-shelled barnacles that attach themselves to their skin. But how to explain mothers escorting their babies right up to people to meet and play with them? The period when mother animals are nursing and raising their babies is usually a time when they are the most shy and protective.

A number of scientists have traveled to Baja over the years to study the friendlies. A wildlife biologist named Dr. Toni Frohoff, an expert in human-dolphin interactions, has been visiting Baja since the late 1990s. She describes the gray whales' behavior there as one of life's most profound mysteries.

A gray whale surfaces near a boat full of tourists in Baja, Mexico.

"It's extraordinary," says Dr. Frohoff. "At precisely the time when you'd expect them to be the most defensive, they're incredibly social. They come right up to boats and let you touch their faces and rub their mouths and give them massages. They behave like it's a great big party."

Dr. Frohoff and other whale scientists have gathered a good bit of evidence suggesting that gray whales are extremely intelligent and have good memories. They also seem very adaptable. A marine biologist at the Natural Resources Defense Council (NRDC) named Elizabeth Alter has found that gray whales change their eating habits depending on what food is available. They seek out new feeding grounds and remember how to find them again. Alter also thinks that many gray whales learned to avoid the Baja lagoons during the peak hunting years and found other places to nurse their young.

Some claim that whales aren't intelligent enough to remember that humans can inflict pain and cause death. But there are many stories of how they avoid certain areas and learn to stay away from trouble spots. So, for a number of scientists, the best explanation for the behavior of the whales in the Baja lagoons is that somehow they have decided it is safe to trust us again.

"It may be that they are forgiving us," says Dr. Frohoff. "But even if it is not that exactly, I believe something very powerful is going on. I'd challenge anybody to say these whales are not actively trying to communicate with humans. Those who reject the idea that whales are intelligent enough to want to interact with us haven't spent enough time around whales."

A gray whale's tail

CHAPTER 6

THE AMAZING WHALE BRAIN

Just how intelligent are whales? The question is very difficult to answer exactly. We can't, of course, speak the whale's language, and even if we could give them some kind of IQ test, it would be based on our idea of what intelligence is, an idea that may not apply at all to how whales think.

We can, however, look at the whale brain for clues as to how smart they are. Whales may live mostly underwater, but they are mammals like us, not fish. Scientists know that many different mammal species, from chimpanzees to elephants to whales, share a number of common features, including certain parts of the brain. By comparing the size and shapes of different mammal brains and by looking at

OPPOSITE PAGE: An orca (a killer whale)

brain tissue and cells under powerful microscopes, scientists can tell a lot about what kind of brainpower a creature has.

❧ THE BIGGEST BRAIN ON EARTH ❧

Scientists at the Mount Sinai School of Medicine in New York City have analyzed the brains of baleen whales such as the humpback and the fin whale. They've studied the brains of many toothed whales as well, like dolphins and killer whales, and the sperm whale. The sperm whale has the largest brain on earth, weighing more than 19 pounds (8.6 kilograms).

The Mount Sinai School of Medicine has a wide collection of different animal brains. They are kept in a giant walk-in refrigerator the size of a small bedroom. The brains sit on metal shelves in glass containers filled with preserving fluid. Along the shelves on one wall there are the brains of gorillas and chimpanzees, spider monkeys, moose, and bats. On the shelves opposite those there is a wide assortment of human brains. Against the back wall of the cooler are the brains of sea creatures: octopuses, dolphins, sharks, and whales.

The sperm whale brain is directly below those in a giant rubber container. It looks like a big white disc about the size of a café table.

The researchers at Mount Sinai found that whale brains have structures surprisingly similar to ours. But when they looked at whale brain tissue under high-powered microscopes, they found something truly amazing.

 SPINDLE CELLS

Inside of our brains there are special, advanced cells known as "spindle cells." They were given this name because they are long rods with bulb-shaped ends that look like the spindles used for spinning wool into thread.

Spindle cells control things like your own awareness of yourself. They allow you to recognize yourself in a mirror. They are also connected to your sense of right and wrong, your emotional attachments to family and friends, and your sense of compassion for others around you. If you are shown a picture of your parents or a picture of someone being hurt, the spindle cells in your brain light up like a pinball machine.

Scientists had long thought that these cells could only be found in our brains. They often referred to spindle cells as "the cells that make us human." And yet here were the

scientists at Mount Sinai staring through their microscopes at great clusters of spindle cells in whales. In fact, they found far more of them in whale brains than we have in ours. And because whales evolved many millions of years before we humans did, whales have had these advanced brain cells far longer than we have.

What could this mean? Could whales be as smart as or even smarter than we are? Do they have strong emotions and feelings of compassion like we do? Are whales aware of being whales? And can they recognize themselves in mirrors?

❧ THE DOLPHIN IN THE MIRROR ❧

We know that one member of the whale family, the dolphin, loves to look at itself in the mirror. A few years ago, a special test was done to find out if dolphins had the brainpower to recognize their own reflection. At the time of the test, only two creatures had shown the ability to do this: humans and our closest biological relative, the chimpanzee. (Elephants have recently shown this ability, too.)

To test if dolphins would respond to their reflection, researchers put big, colorful paint dots on the backs of dolphins who were being kept in large swimming tanks. The colorful dots were placed just behind each dolphin's head. The only way they could see the dots would be by looking at an underwater mirror that was attached to the side of the tank.

The researchers held their breath and watched. Sure enough, one by one, the dolphins approached the mirror. As they swam by, they noticed the strange dots on their backs and then returned to the mirror so they could examine the spots more closely. Over and over they did this, as though they were fascinated by their own reflections, as though they couldn't get enough of themselves.

It would be tough to get a mirror big enough for a sperm whale or a blue whale to look into. And we can't study whale brains while they are actually working the way we can study our own. We can't tell, for example, if a whale's spindle cells light up when they see their own family members or when they see another whale being injured by a harpoon.

But the very fact that their brains contain so many spindle cells is a good sign that there is a lot going on inside the heads of whales. Beyond this, perhaps the best way to get a sense of what whales might think and feel is just from watching how they behave. In fact, the longer and closer we look at whales, the more we are, just like those dolphins in the mirror test, seeing clear reflections of ourselves.

It is difficult to observe large whales like gray whales or sperm whales for long periods of time. But sometimes we are offered a rare chance to have a great big wild whale living right beside us each day. One stranded gray whale that was rescued in southern California touched the hearts of people around the world and gave us exciting new information about whale brains and whale behavior.

❧ THE STORY OF J.J. ❧

Back in January 1997, a week-old, 14-foot-long (4.3-meter-long) baby female gray whale was found on the beaches of Marina del Rey, California, north of San Diego. It was never determined how or why the baby whale got stranded, but she was so hungry that her skull and ribs could be seen under her skin. Volunteers were able to push her back out to sea, hoping she would join with other gray whales swimming south toward the Baja lagoons. But the next morning, she was found floating in a nearby channel, close to death.

The baby, nicknamed J.J., was lifted onto a truck and driven south to SeaWorld, a marine wildlife park in San

Diego. The plan was to slowly nurture her back to health and release her into the wild. This had been done only once before with a captive gray whale, so no one knew what to expect.

J.J. was put in a special square tank, 40 feet (12.2 meters) on each side. At the start she was fed fluids to prevent dehydration and antibiotics to keep her from getting infections. As J.J. began to recover, she was given a special formula made of cream, blended fish, and vitamins, as close as we could make to real mother whale milk. After months of that, her diet was changed to fish. J.J. was soon being fed 500 pounds (227 kilograms) of fish a day, everything from krill to squid to sardines. By her fourteenth month, J.J. had grown to be 30 feet (9.1 meters) long and to weigh 18,000 pounds (8,165 kilograms). This made her the largest marine mammal ever in captivity.

Having a gray whale in captivity was a rare learning opportunity for scientists. During J.J.'s first spring at SeaWorld, for example, she was always found floating off to one side of her tank. The caretakers feared that this might be a sign that J.J. was bored and depressed. Then it occurred to them that she was facing north, the direction of the gray whales' spring migration back to their feeding grounds in the Bering Sea. A short time later, studies of gray whale brains revealed that they actually have tiny particles of iron in their brain tissue that respond to the earth's magnetic forces. Whales, in other words, have their own built-in guidance systems.

J.J.'s stay at SeaWorld also allowed a team of Russian scientists to conduct the first sleep studies on whales. Monitoring J.J.'s brain activity while she slept, they produced evidence that whales do, in fact, dream!

J.J. RETURNS HOME

By the time J.J.'s planned date of release arrived in the early spring of 1998, millions of people around the world were following the story. Police closed the freeways so that she could be driven to her release spot off San Diego's Point Loma. A construction crane was needed to lift J.J.—now 31 feet (9.4 meters) long and 19,200 pounds (8,709 kilograms)—onto a Coast Guard vessel called the *Conifer*. Coast Guard helicopters, meanwhile, flew above the waters off Point Loma, looking for gray whales migrating north that J.J. could join up with. Researchers also attached radio transmitters to J.J.'s side so that they could track her progress.

When a group of migrating whales was spotted, J.J. was hoisted off the *Conifer*'s deck in a harness and set gently down into the sea. As she was released, the first question on everyone's mind was, would she even know which way to swim? J.J., after all, had not been in contact with another whale for most of her life and so had no way of learning from adults of her own species.

Everyone held their breath and watched as J.J. swam free of her harness. She circled a few times. Then she dove out of sight. Two days later, all radio contact was lost. Researchers figure that J.J. probably scraped the transmitters off against the ocean floor. The last anyone saw of her, she was not far from San Diego, near the Mexican border. But she was near a group of other whales, and all were heading north.

It's impossible to say now whether J.J. is still alive or what she looks like as a full-grown adult. There have been many rumors in recent years that she is among the "friendlies" who come to Baja each year. Some say she has now raised many calves of her own. We don't know for sure what became of J.J. But we do know a lot more about her world, thanks to her brief stay in ours.

CHAPTER 7

WHAT WHALES CAN DO

Even the most brutal whale hunters could sense that they were chasing after intelligent animals. As the hunting of sperm whales was reaching its peak in the 1800s, more and more stories began to appear about whales fighting back against their attackers. It wasn't just individual whales. They would work together as a team, either on defense or offense. Adults would gather the calves together and then form a tight protective circle around them, their heads pressed together, nose-to-nose, looking in at the babies.

If you saw such formations from above, they would resemble giant flowers, the whales' tail fins, or "flukes," thrashing like petals in the wind. Sometimes, the whales

OPPOSITE PAGE: A humpback whale breaching

would turn the formation inside out, so that their flukes were at the center of the circle, nearest the calves and their heads were facing outward, toward their attackers. This is a perfect example of what is known as a complex cooperative strategy. Only highly intelligent creatures are capable of this sort of behavior.

〜 ATTACK OF THE ANGRY WHALES 〜

One of the best-known stories of such cooperation among whales was told by a Nantucket whaler named Owen Chase back in 1821. Chase was on board the whaling ship *Essex* in the South Pacific when the ship was charged by a large, adult-male sperm whale.

According to Chase, the whale was angry at seeing his fellow whales attacked and came at the *Essex* at "twice his ordinary speed." With one huge blow of the whale's head into the back of the ship, the *Essex* was sunk. The crew quickly scrambled into lifeboats. They began to row away, but all at once they found themselves surrounded by a tight circle of sperm whales "blowing and spouting at a terrible rate."

Darkness fell. The men sat frozen in terror, listening all through the night to the sound of angry whales, their flukes churning up the sea. There were islands nearby, but rumors of cannibals prevented the men from trying to reach them. Over the coming days, the whales continued to swim in circles around the lifeboats. The crew just drifted there in place, slowly dying of thirst and starvation. Finally, another large whaling ship arrived to rescue them. The story of the *Essex* was the inspiration behind Herman Melville's famous novel *Moby-Dick*.

STEALING FISH RIGHT OFF THE HOOK

To this day, whales often outsmart even modern fishermen who have no interest in catching whales. Scientists recently managed to get incredible underwater videos of giant sperm whales stealing from fishermen's lines in Alaska. Somehow, these whales have figured out how to use their massive jaws to pluck the caught fish right off the hook. It looks like they're eating little appetizers off a toothpick.

Fishermen are losing as much as 10 percent of their fish each year to whales. They also fear the problem is getting worse, because the whales who have learned the fish-stealing technique are teaching it to others. In fact, the news seems to have spread to other sperm whales far and wide. Reports of stolen fish are coming in now from fishermen all over the world!

🌊 FISHING WITH BUBBLE NETS 🌊

And just when you think you've heard it all, we now know that whales fish with their own nets. Whales, in fact, invented the concept. After 20 years spent observing humpback whales, a scientist from the Alaska Whale Foundation named Fred Sharpe has figured out their brilliant strategy. A group of humpbacks will get together and begin to produce a series of hunting calls. The calls have a pure, high, ringing

tone that the whales use to drive fish toward the ocean's surface. While this is happening, the leader of the humpback group will dive down underneath the fish and shoot an intense stream of air bubbles from its blow hole. The bubbles rise toward the surface, surrounding the fish, causing them to gather together as though trapped in a huge net. When this bubble net has caught as many fish as possible, the whole group of humpbacks rises up toward the surface with their mouths open wide.

The humpbacks' invention of bubble nets is a clear example of the use of a tool. The use of tools was long thought to be, like spindle cells, what made us humans different from all the other animals. Now, however, we know this isn't true. A number of different creatures, including chimps, elephants, and, of course, whales, have enough brains to invent tools and to use them together for a common purpose.

⁓ FROM WHALE TO WHALE TO WHALE ⁓

Whales also do something else that we used to think only humans could do. They communicate the news of their inventions to others in their group, and they pass along this knowledge to their young as well. Sharing knowledge among members of a community and passing it along to the next generation is the very definition of the word *culture*. Whales not only invented fishing with nets before we did— they, like chimps and elephants, invented culture before we did, too.

Hal Whitehead, a marine biologist based in Nova Scotia, Canada, has been studying sperm whales for nearly 30 years. He follows them in his boat on their migratory routes around the world. Over the years, Whitehead has come to realize that sperm whales have social structures just as huge and complex as their brains. The whales are members of social groups or "clans" that have many thousands of members and wander over thousands of miles of ocean. The whales of a clan are not all related. But within the larger clans, there are smaller, close-knit family groups. The immediate family is surrounded and supported by grandparents, aunts, and uncles. They all help in raising and educating the young, teaching them how to communicate and navigate and hunt.

"They are living in these massive, elaborate undersea societies," Whitehead says. "It is sort of strange, really. The closest thing to compare it to would be ourselves."

It all makes you think again about those songs of the humpbacks. And the conga drumming of the gray whales. And the loud clicks of the sperm whales. And the long, low, ocean-wide moans of the massive blue whales. It makes you wonder what it is exactly that they are saying to one another down there . . . and whether they might even be talking sometimes about us.

Humpback whales

CHAPTER 8

SOUND and the WHALE

Sound is the whale's most vital tool. Think of how hard it is to see underwater, even when you are in the clearest swimming pool. It is much harder to see in the ocean. Average visibility is at most about 10 feet (3 meters). Whales, therefore, are almost entirely dependent upon sound and their sense of hearing to survive in their world. This is why the part of their brain that controls hearing is 10 times larger than it is in the human brain.

Fortunately, sound travels faster and farther through water than it does through the air. This not only makes the ocean the whales' great chat room, but also allows whales to use sound in order to see. Whales can tell, for example, the

OPPOSITE PAGE: A beluga whale

depth of the water they are in by the changes in the sounds they hear around them. When the shore is near and the water shallower, sounds will be higher pitched and faster. As the water gets deeper farther from land, sounds slow down and grow deeper as well.

This is especially true when whales are in a more contained body of water like the lagoons of Baja. The lagoons are surrounded by land on three sides with little openings out into the wider Pacific. Whales know the "soundscape" of these lagoons the way we know the landscapes of our hometowns. They hear how different the lagoon sounds when strong winds blow across the water's surface, or when rain beats down on it, or when boat motors are approaching. They hear anything and everything that affects the sound of the world they live in.

This is true not only in lagoons. Whales can also hear changes in the wide-open ocean. Blue, fin, and humpback whales can actually hear how the structure of the sea is changed by the presence of a large island like Bermuda. They hear the different sound of the warm Gulf Stream currents as they flow north through the colder northern oceans. And they can tell the sound of a giant patch of swimming krill, the little shrimplike creatures that are one of the main food sources for many whales. Krill patches can be as large as 20 miles (32.2 kilometers) long and 100 feet (30.5 meters) wide. Blue whales hear the krill making their way through the water and swim straight toward them with their mouths wide open.

🐚 WHALE TALK 🐚

Just as whales can hear changes to their watery underworld, they can change the ways in which they talk. Scientists have so far identified eight different sounds made by the gray whales in Baja, Mexico. Along with the rhythmic pounding of the conga drum, the gray whale's most common call, their vocabulary also includes croaks, moans, and grunts. The great fin whale, meanwhile, emits long, steady sequences of pulses that register at the very limit of our hearing ability. The sound is so common in the sea that for many years divers mistakenly thought it was the creaking of the ocean floor. As for what all these different sounds might mean—nobody has been able to figure that out just yet.

❧ DIFFERENT CLICKS FOR EVERY CLAN ❧

CLICK!
CLICK!
CLICK!

If you listen to the sperm whale's loud clicking noises underwater, they sound very much like the electronic dots and dashes of Morse code signals. Aside from navigating and hunting for food, it isn't quite clear what other information sperm whales are communicating to one another with their clicking language. But Hal Whitehead, the sperm whale specialist in Nova Scotia (mentioned on page 84), has made some fascinating discoveries about sperm whale speech.

It turns out that those huge, many-thousand-member clans that sperm whales belong to each have their own unique pattern of clicking. Just as people from a certain region of the world have their own version of a language, or dialect, so do sperm whales. Whitehead has positively identified five

CLICK!
CLICK!

different dialects so far. He has studied two of them closely
and has learned their patterns.

CLICK!
CLICK!
CLICK!

"There are regular clans," Whitehead explains. "They
make anywhere from three to eight equally spaced clicks. And
then there are what I call the 'Plus-One' clans. They have two
to eight clicks and then a pause and then an added click on
the end, kind of like when someone says, 'you know' after
every sentence."

Whitehead has also noticed that different clans swim
through the water differently. The regular clans move in
wiggly tracks closer to the shore, while the Plus-Ones swim
farther out to sea and in straighter lines. The reason for these
differences is not quite clear.

CLICK!
CLICK!
CLICK!

HUMPBACK CHATTERS, SIRENS, AND MELODIES

A good deal has also been learned about the language of the humpbacks in the 40 years since their songs became a worldwide recording sensation and then got launched into outer space. Humpbacks, we now know, have a variety of languages. There are the so-called "social sounds," used to communicate with one another when they're traveling. There are the cooing and chattering sounds made between mothers and their newborn calves. And then there is what is known as the "feeding siren," sounded when the humpbacks reach their feeding grounds, sort of like the ringing of our dinner bell.

As for their famous songs, scientists have learned that only the male humpbacks sing and that they do so mostly in breeding grounds. It seems as if they're singing love songs in hope of attracting a mate! The songs last anywhere from five to twenty minutes. They don't have melodies like our love songs, but they do have phrases that get repeated as themes, much like our classical music compositions. Whales not only invented net fishing, language, and culture before us—but musical composition as well!

Every year more studies are being conducted on whales and their unique languages. Who knows what new discoveries we'll be making about them in the future—if, that is, we can still hear them, and they can still hear each other.

It so happens that just as we humans are beginning to appreciate whale language and song, we are also in danger of drowning them all out with our own noises.

Before human beings were around, blue whales in the Arctic were able to talk and sing to blue whales in Antarctica. Sperm whales could trade messages across oceans. Humpbacks, and grays, and fins, and all the rest, had only other whale chatter and songs to compete with. Now, however, everywhere they turn, they hear us. The sounds of giant ship tanker engines, the motors of recreational boating, and the new, high-pitched echoes of military sonar devices are filling the whales' worldwide chat room with so much noise, we might soon be driving all of them right out of their minds.

CHAPTER 9

OUR NOISE *in* THEIR WORLD

On the afternoon of September 25, 2002, a group of marine biologists vacationing on San Jose Island, off the coast of Baja, Mexico, came upon a couple of stranded whales. A quick check of their bodies revealed that the whales had died recently. The scientists radioed a nearby marine-mammal laboratory. A scientist came to the beach to do an examination. He identified the victims as beaked whales.

BEAKED WHALE

Relatively small members of the whale family, beaked whales resemble large dolphins. They are not often seen, and very little is known about them because they are such deep swimmers. And yet oddly enough, just one day before the stranding of the pair on San Jose Island, 14 beaked whales had been found stranded along the beaches of the Canary Islands off the northwestern coast of Africa. Those whales were found still alive, and yet all efforts by rescuers to save them failed, and the whales soon died.

It seemed strange to have two sets of beaked whales strand themselves within 24 hours of each other on opposite sides of the world. Still, it was difficult to make any connection between the two events.

There are many theories about why whales strand themselves. Some think that the leader of a whale group might get sick and disoriented, and all the others in the group follow it when it strays off course. Others think that whales can get confused by sudden shallow stretches of shore along their migration routes. It turns out, however, that there was one very interesting common connection between the stranding incidents in the Canary Islands and on San Jose Island.

❧ SONAR AND AIR GUNS ❧

The rescuers in the Canary Islands noticed that there were a number of navy ships using high-tech sonar tracking devices that day in military training exercises not far offshore. Such exercises had been connected with four other previous strandings of beaked whales on Canary Island beaches since 1985. And while there were no military exercises being conducted off the shore of San Jose Island, there was a research ship out on the water that day, using powerful underwater air guns. The guns make extremely loud noises to test the ocean floor for signs of oil and gas deposits.

Whale scientists had suspected for years that whale stranding incidents could be connected with loud noises like those from sonar or underwater air guns. Scientists had examined the bodies of stranded whales all over the world and found bleeding around the whales' brains and ears. Their eardrums and brain tissue had actually been ruptured by the power of the noise. But the examinations done on the whales that stranded in the Canary Islands revealed something else even more shocking.

🌊 DRIVEN TO THE SURFACE 🌊

There is a painful condition that human beings sometimes suffer known as "the bends." It is caused when people who have been deep underwater, where there is a lot of pressure, come up to the surface too quickly (usually while scuba diving). Their bodies don't have time to adjust to the lighter pressure near the surface, and as a result, their organs begin to rupture and bleed. They also develop tiny nitrogen bubbles in their organ tissue, one of the telltale signs of the bends.

Of course, the bends is about the last thing scientists would expect a whale to suffer from. Whales spend nearly all their lives deep underwater, rising up to the surface every 10 to 20 minutes to grab a breath of air. No creature is more skilled at dealing with changing water pressures than the whale. And yet while examining the stranded Canary

Island whales, scientists found not only bleeding around their brains and ears. They also found ruptured livers, lungs, and kidneys, and nitrogen bubbles everywhere. The whales had suffered from the bends.

Suddenly, the cause of the stranding became clear. The whales had been so disturbed by the navy's new sonar that, to get away from the sound, they raced to the surface too quickly.

In the years following the Canary Island strandings, other stranded whales were found with similar injuries. The conclusion was no longer possible to avoid.

⚓ THE NOISY OCEAN ⚓

Only 150 years ago, the seas remained mostly free of human sounds. With the invention of the diesel engine, however, all that began to change. Today, the engine of one modern supertanker (a ship more than two football fields long) can be heard far across the sea. Now think of the sound of the tens of thousands of these tankers and cargo ships traveling the world's oceans at any one time. Add to those all the barges, icebreakers, ocean liners, tugboats, ferries, and motorboats, and you can begin to understand how thick the massive fog of our noise has become.

Ships, however, are only part of the problem. Everywhere now companies are exploring for new undersea oil and gas deposits. From the back of their search boats, powerful air guns shoot tens of thousands of blasts strong enough to penetrate deep rock layers beneath the ocean's floor. And when oil is discovered, more explosives are required both to set up drilling platforms and to remove them later. There is just no end to the sounds of human industry. Noise pollution has become so widespread that many researchers now say that when they put their microphones underwater, they can no longer hear whale songs. They hear only us.

Still, of all the different human sounds now echoing through the whales' world, by far the most damaging is sonar. Countries around the world are now using high-intensity sonar to detect and track submarines. As a result, the number of whale stranding incidents is increasing.

⚞ SHOULD WE BAN SONAR? ⚟

The problem has gotten so bad that concerned people have made efforts to ban the use of sonar in order to protect marine life. In one very important case, the NRDC and a number of environmental groups sued the U.S. Navy over its use of sonar. The environmentalists ended up winning two big battles in the California court when judges decided to heavily restrict the navy's use of sonar in its training exercises.

In November 2008, the case finally came before the United States Supreme Court. The navy won that round— the court ruled against the restrictions on the use of sonar. But even though it won the case, the navy made an agreement with the NRDC to scout the areas where it is about to do training exercises in order to avoid using sonar when whales are nearby.

Too often our respect for other creatures only comes at the cost of nearly destroying them. But we may now finally be reaching a turning point in our long, violent relationship with whales. There is no longer such a clear boundary between our world and theirs. We have learned too much about them—about their brains, their behavior, their language, their culture—to pretend that they don't matter to us.

The big question now is, have we learned these things too late? Can we continue to pursue our way of life while also making way for whales? There are some positive signs that we can, but it is all up to us. We are the only ones with the power and, hopefully, the imagination to make it happen.

A humpback whale mother and calf

CONCLUSION

Every late winter, Pacific gray whales make the long, hard journey from their feeding grounds in the far northern Bering Sea (near Alaska) to the warm lagoons of Baja, Mexico. By late spring, after months of nursing their newborn calves, the gray whales leave the lagoons and start north again.

The world's whales have been making these same migrations for millions of years. We've been able to keep a close watch on the gray whale's journey because they stay close to shore as they go. This also makes their trip particularly tough because they are more likely to be disturbed by us: loud tankers and cargo ships, navy sonar exercises, and thousands and thousands of smaller boats motoring back and forth. The problem has gotten so serious that a number of whale researchers and conservationists are now working to create a boat-free zone exclusively for the whales. It would be called the "whale's lane."

Thousands of years ago, in the mythology of ancient Iceland, the ocean was called the "whale road." Now we may soon be turning that imaginary road into an actual one. This is just one sign that our attitude toward whales may finally be changing. If we can begin to make way for the gray whales amidst all our traffic along the West Coast, perhaps we can do the same for the world's other whales.

❧ WHY WHALES MATTER SO MUCH ☙

Whales are important to us not only because they are extremely intelligent beings who share our planet with us. They are also important because the overall health of whales also tells us about the health of the planet.

In the old days, coal miners would take a caged canary with them down into the mine shaft. If the canary passed out or died, the miners knew that they didn't have enough healthy air to breathe in the shaft. Well, whales have become for us like the canary in the coal mine. If they can no longer live and prosper in the seas, then we know those seas are very sick and in need of our attention.

That is why saving whales is the same as saving the planet and ourselves. We are all in this together.

⚡ GIVING BACK TO WHALES ⚡

Now, thanks to everyone from scientists to conservationists to a growing number of whale watchers, we are finally finding ways to give back to the whales. Along with the efforts to create a "whale's lane," people are keeping close track of yearly whale migrations, doing careful counts of their populations, and watching out for stray or injured whales. And now more people than ever before are going out on the water not to hunt whales, but simply to watch and marvel at them.

There are many things we still don't know or understand about whales. Much more research needs to be done into both whale behavior and language. Some things about them will always remain a mystery. We can never know, for example, what a whale thinks or feels, or what a whale's day is really like. But thanks to the latest scientific discoveries, we do know now for certain that whales have complex and busy days of their own. They display joy and anger and sadness. They use tools and teach fellow whales how to use them. They swim and hunt and play together in large social groups, and they speak to each other in their own language. Whales not only have self-awareness, they also seem to be highly aware of us and our actions as well.

Just ask the group of professional scuba divers who were called out on a strange sea-rescue mission five years ago. In December 2005, a female humpback whale was spotted off the coast of San Francisco, struggling to stay afloat. The whale was tangled up in a web of crab traps. Hundreds of yards of nylon rope were wrapped around her mouth, body, and tail. When the divers arrived in their boat, they could see that the only way to save the whale would be to jump in and try to cut her loose.

FISHING GEAR

A humpback whale entangled in fishing gear

It took them over an hour to cut all the lines. They had to move very carefully, knowing that one swipe of the whale's tail could easily drown them. But she held still the whole time. When she was finally freed, she swam around for a while in circles. The divers watched nervously, not knowing what to expect. And then the huge whale came back and paid a visit to each of the divers. She came up and gently nudged them, one by one, as if to say thanks. And then she swam away.

The divers said later that it was one of the most moving experiences they'd ever had. As for the diver who cut the lines around the whale's mouth, he said that the whole time he was working, her huge eye was right there, watching him, following his every move, trusting him to help her. The experience, he said, changed his life forever.